THE LITIGANTS

By JEAN RACINE

Translated by ROBERT BRUCE BOSWELL

A Digireads.com Book
Digireads.com Publishing

The Litigants
By Jean Racine
Translated by Robert Bruce Boswell
ISBN 10: 1-4209-4909-8
ISBN 13: 978-1-4209-4909-4

Please visit *www.digireads.com*

THE LITIGANTS.

A Comedy.

INTRODUCTION TO THE LITIGANTS.

This play, which is neither a comedy nor a farce but has elements in common with each, was first performed in 1668 at Paris, and afterwards at Versailles. Its humour in a great measure depends upon the mock gravity which masks its ridiculous features; the language and style are those of comedy, while the tone of exaggeration and the absurdity of the situations belong more fitly to burlesque. It is a French adaptation of "The Wasps" of Aristophanes, to which the wit of Rabelais and of Furetière (author of the "Roman Bourgeois") have contributed not a little. Racine's own experience of law and lawyers was derived from the suit in which he had been involved about the Priory of Epernay, during the course of which he picked up a number of barbarous terms, "which," to quote his own words, "neither my judges nor I ever properly understood."

"Les Plaideurs," though it fell rather flat at first, has proved to be by far the most popular of all Racine's plays.

CHARACTERS.

DANDIN, *a judge.*
LEANDER, *son of Dandin,*
CHICANEAU, *a citizen.*
ISABELLE, *daughter of Chicaneau.*
A Countess.
PETIT-JEAN, *a house porter.*
L'INTIMÉ, *a clerk.*
A Prompter.

The scene is laid in a town of Lower Normandy.

THE LITIGANTS.

A COMEDY.

ACT I.

SCENE I.

PETIT-JEAN. [*hauling along a big bag full of raw-papers.*]
    Oh, what a fool is he who trusts the future:
    Who laughs at morn will cry before the night.
    A judge took me, last year, into his service,—
    Fetch'd me from Amiens to be Swiss porter.
    These Normans thought to laugh at my expense:
    When we're with wolves, one learns to howl, they say.
    I played a wily hand, tho' a poor Picard,
    And crack'd my whip loudly as any other.
    All the fine gentlemen would, hat in hand,
    Call me good Mr. Petit-Jean, with flatteries
    Long as your arm. But honours without coin
    Are naught. I acted like a play-house porter;
    In vain they knock'd, and bow'd with heads uncover'd,
    Save with the silver key, they might not enter.
    No money,—then no Swiss, to unlock the door.
    'Tis true my master's pocket took a scantling;
    Sometimes there came a reckoning. 'Twas my charge
    To purchase hay, and candles for the house;
    I did not lose by that, at all events;
    I might have bought the straw into the bargain.
    His heart was too much in his work, however,—
    The more's the pity,—first in court, and last,
    Each day, and often quite alone; believe me,
    He'd like to sleep there without sup or morsel.
    I'd say at times,—"Dear Mr. Perrin Dandin,
    Excuse my freedom, you get up too early.
    He who would travel far should spare his steed;
    Drink, eat, and sleep, and make a fire to last."
    He took no heed. And so well have his vigils
    Repaid him, that they say his brain is crack'd.
    One up, one down, he wants to judge us all.
    He's always mumbling some strange gibberish,
    I know not what, and will, by hook or crook,
    Take with him into bed his wig and gown.
    He had his cock killed, in a fit of rage,
    Because it didn't wake him up in time:
    He said, a suitor, whose affair went ill,
    Had with a bribe corrupted the poor bird.

Poor man, this sentence did him little good,
His son all talk of business has tabooed:
He makes us guard him closely night and day,
Or else,—good-bye, he's off, and in the court!
Heav'n knows, he's quick enough to give the slip.
And I,—no sleep for me, I'm growing thin,
Wretchedly thin; I stretch my arms and yawn.
But watch who will, this bag shall be my pillow:
To-night, i' faith, I'll take my ease for once!
No one can blame me sleeping in the streets.
Let's go to sleep.

[*He lies down on the ground.*]

SCENE II. L'INTIMÉ, PETIT-JEAN.

L'INTIMÉ. What ho! Friend Petit-Jean!
PETIT-JEAN. L'Intimé!
    [*aside.*] He's afraid I'm catching cold.
L'INTIMÉ. My stars! What brings you in the street so early?
PETIT-JEAN. I'm not a stork, to stand upon one leg,
    For ever on the watch, hearing him shout.
    What bellows too! I think the man's possess'd.
L'INTIMÉ. Excellent!
PETIT-JEAN. When I scratch my head, and tell him
    I'd like to go to sleep, he gravely says,—
    "Lodge a petition how you wish to sleep."
    It makes me sleepy but to talk of it.
    Good night.
L'INTIMÉ. Good night, forsooth! Deuce take it, if—
    But hark, I think I hear a noise up there.

SCENE III. DANDIN, L'INTIMÉ, PETIT-JEAN.

DANDIN. [*at the window.*] Petit-Jean! L'Intimé!
L'INTIMÉ. [*to* PETIT-JEAN.] Hush!
DANDIN. I'm alone.
    My keepers prove defaulters, Heav'n be prais'd.
    Give time enough, they'll enter an appearance.
    Now for a gaol delivery thro' the window.
    Out of the court there!
L'INTIMÉ. Ha! Well jump'd!
PETIT-JEAN. You're caught, Sir!
DANDIN. Thieves! Thieves!
PETIT-JEAN. We've got you now, and won't let go.
L'INTIMÉ. There's no good bawling.
DANDIN. Help! They're murdering me!

SCENE IV. LEANDER, DANDIN, L'INTIMÉ, PETIT-JEAN.

LEANDER. I hear my father in the street. Quick, lights!
    Father, what brings you out at such an hour?
    Whither away so fast?
DANDIN. I want to judge.
LEANDER. Judge whom? The world's asleep.
PETIT-JEAN. Except myself.
LEANDER. Why, what a heap of bags! They're all about him.
DANDIN. It will be quite three months ere I come back,
    And these are my provisions,—bags and papers.
LEANDER. But you'll want food.
DANDIN. There's a refreshment stall.
LEANDER. Where will you sleep then, father?
DANDIN. On the bench.
LEANDER. No, father; you'd much better stay at home.
    Lie in your own bed, eat at your own table.
    Listen to reason, and let that persuade you;
    And for your health—
DANDIN. I like to be unwell.
LEANDER. You're bad enough already. Take some rest:
    You'll soon be nothing but mere skin and bones.
DANDIN. Best? Would you have me rule myself by you?
    Think you a judge has nought to do but pace
    The streets like any fop, and make good cheer,
    Gambling by day, and dancing all the night?
    No, money does not drop into one's hands;
    Each of your ribbands costs me an award,
    Yet you're asham'd to be a judge's son,
    And ape the nobleman. Dandin, my friend,
    See the ancestral portraits on my walls,
    All of them wearing the judicial robes;
    No other line is half so good; compare
    A judge's fees with what a marquis gets;
    Wait till the year's end, and then count our gains.
    A nobleman's no better than a pillar
    Inside my hall! The smartest swell among them
    Will stand there blowing on his frozen fingers,
    His nose close muffled, or a hand thrust down
    Into his pocket; and to warm himself
    He'll turn my spit. That's how they fare. Poor boy,
    Your angel mother never taught you so.
    My Babonnette, I weep to think of her,
    How not a single sitting she would miss,
    How all her life she never left my side,
    And took away full often Heav'n knows what:
    She would have rather pocketed the napkins

The waiter brought, than gone home empty-handed,
That's how to raise a family! Begone;
You're nothing but a fool.
LEANDER. You'll soon catch cold
If you stand there. Take him back, Petit-Jean,
Put him to bed, shut every door and window,
Making all fast, and keep your master warm.
PETIT-JEAN. You must have stronger railings fix'd up there.
DANDIN. What! go to bed thus without legal forms!
First get an order sign'd how I'm to sleep.
LEANDER. Lie down at least, pending proceedings, father.
DANDIN. I'll go; but mark me, to enrage you all
I will not sleep a wink.
LEANDER. All well and good!
Don't let him be alone. Stay, L'Intimé.

SCENE V. LEANDER, L'INTIMÉ.

LEANDER. I wish to have some words with you in private.
L'INTIMÉ. *You'll* need a keeper next.
LEANDER. I need one now.
Alas, I'm quite as crazy as my father.
L'INTIMÉ. You want to judge?
LEANDER. [*pointing to Isabelle's dwelling.*] Enough of mystery!
You know that house there.
L'INTIMÉ. Now I understand you.
'Tis early in the day to go a-courting.
You want me to discuss Miss Isabelle;
I've told you often she's discreet and pretty;
But then consider Chicaneau, her father,
Consumes in lawsuits well-nigh all her fortune.
He sues each man he meets. I think he'll bring
All France before the bar ere he has done.
He's taken lodgings next door to his judge,
One would be always pleading, and the other
Still on the bench; nor will your case be settled
Till he has sued you all, priest, lawyer, bridegroom.
LEANDER. I know't as well as you; in spite of all
I die for Isabelle.
L'INTIMÉ. Well, marry her.
You only have to speak, and it is done.
LEANDER. Not quite so soon as you imagine. No,
Her father is a Tartar, and I dread him.
Unless you are an usher or attorney,
One may not see his daughter. She, poor girl,
Shut up at home, as in a prison, mourns
While youth is spent in vain regrets, her portion
In lawsuits, and my passion's flame in smoke.

Yes, he will ruin her, if this goes on.
Now don't you know some honest forger fellow
Who'll serve his friend—for a consideration,—
Some zealous bailiff?
L'INTIMÉ. There are plenty of them!
LEANDER. Still to be had?
L'INTIMÉ. Ah, Sir, if my poor father
Were yet alive, he'd be the man to suit you.
He made more in one day, than would another
In six months. On his wrinkled brow were writ
His exploits. He'd have stopp'd a prince's carriage,
And taken him himself. He pocketed
Nineteen of every twenty lashes given
In the whole province. I'm my father's son;
How can I help you?
LEANDER. You?
L'INTIMÉ. Ay, better, maybe,
Than any bailiff.
LEANDER. Would you serve her father
With a false writ?
L'INTIMÉ. H'm.
LEANDER. Give the girl a letter?
L'INTIMÉ. Both in my line. Why not?
LEANDER. Hark! Someone calls. We'll think of this some other time.

SCENE VI. CHICANEAU, PETIT-JEAN.

CHICANEAU. [*going away and then corning back.*] La Brie,
Secure the house well, I shall soon return.
Let no one mount the stairs while I'm away.
See that this letter's sent by next mail southward.
Go and choose three fine rabbits from the hutches,
And take them this forenoon to my attorney.
If his clerk comes, give him a glass of wine,
And let him have that bag beside my window.
I wonder if that's all. Oh! should there call
A tall, thin man,—you know him, serves as witness
And swears for me at need—asking to see me,
Tell him to wait. The judge I fear's gone out,
It's nearly four. But I will knock.
PETIT-JEAN. [*half-opening the door.*] Who's there?
CHICANEAU. I wish to see your master.
PETIT-JEAN. [*shutting the door.*] Not at home.
CHICANEAU. [*knocking at the door.*]
His secretary, can I speak a word to him?
PETIT-JEAN. [*shutting the door.*]
No.
CHICANEAU. [*knocking again.*] Well, his porter?

PETIT-JEAN. I am he.

CHICANEAU. Pray drink
My health, Sir.

PETIT-JEAN. [*taking money.*] Much good may it do you!
[*shutting the door.*] But
Return to-morrow.

CHICANEAU. Give me back my money.
In truth the world is getting sadly wicked.
I've known the time when lawsuits gave no trouble!
Six crowns well spent would win me half-a-dozen.
It seems to me my whole estate to-day
Would hardly be enough to bribe a porter.
But I perceive the Countess of Pimbesche
Approaches, surely on some pressing business.

SCENE VII. THE COUNTESS, CHICANEAU.

CHICANEAU. There's no admittance, Ma'am.

THE COUNTESS. Didn't I say so?
I faith my lackeys make me lose my senses.
Scold as I will, they won't get up for me;
And all the household sleeps till I awake it.

CHICANEAU. He must have told his servant to deny him.

THE COUNTESS. I've tried to get a word with him these two days,
But all in vain.

CHICANEAU. My adversary's strong,
And makes me fear.

THE COUNTESS. After *my* treatment, *you,* Sir,
Must not complain.

CHICANEAU. Right's on my side, however.

THE COUNTESS. Ah! what injustice!

CHICANEAU. I appeal to you, Ma'am.

THE COUNTESS. Sir, you should know the shameful treachery—

CHICANEAU. A trivial cause at bottom—

THE COUNTESS. Let me tell you—

CHICANEAU. The facts are these. Some twenty years ago
A certain donkey cross'd a field of mine,
Roll'd in the grass, and did a lot of damage;
Against him then I lodged an information,
Had him arrested, and an arbitrator
Named. At two trusses he assess'd the damage
Done to the hay. A year pass'd by, and then
I found myself non-suited, and appeal'd.
They sued upon the judgment, till the case
Came on for hearing,—Madam, mark this well—
Drolichon—let me tell you he's no fool,—
Gets, at some cost, a judgment on request.
And so I gain my case. What happens then?

The trickster on his side stops execution.
Meanwhile another incident occurs;
Defendant's fowl invades the self-same meadow,—
Order of Court to draw up a report
Of how much hay a hen can eat a day,—
Added to previous case. Things being thus
"In statu quo," the hearing is referr'd
To April eighth or ninth, year fifty-six.
I take fresh action, furnish and procure
Pleas, declarations, arguments, and warrants,
Experts' reports, injunctions, writs of error,
Statements of grievance, and fresh evidence,
With affidavits, royal letters patent,
And confutations. Then a dozen rules,
And writs are issued; we produce new proofs,
And replications follow. Judgment giv'n,—
I lose my case with costs—three hundred pounds
To pay! Is that the justice of the law?
And after twenty years! I've one resource left;
The Court of Chancery is open to me.
I won't give in. But you, as I perceive,
Have a suit pending?
THE COUNTESS. Would to Heav'n I had!
CHICANEAU. I'll burn my boats!
THE COUNTESS. I—
CHICANEAU. Pay three hundred pounds!
    All for a truss or two of hay!
THE COUNTESS. My lawsuits
    Have all been stopp'd, tho' there were only left
    Four or five little ones—against my husband,
    My father, and my children. Oh! the pity of it!
    They spared no dirty trick that could be thought of.
    Nor was that all; they've got a judge's order
    By which I am restrain'd,—my food and clothing
    Provided me,—from going to law again.
    CHICANEAU. From going to law?
THE COUNTESS. Yes, Sir, from going to law.
CHICANEAU. That's monstrous!
THE COUNTESS. Sir, I'm driven to despair.
CHICANEAU. To tie the hands of such a noble lady!
    But the allowance, Madam, is it large?
THE COUNTESS. 'Twould keep me very comfortably, Sir.
    But life is worthless without going to law.
CHICANEAU. Shall knaves then eat us up, body and soul,
    And we say nothing? Tell me, please, how long
    It is since you began.
THE COUNTESS. I can't remember,
    'Tis thirty years or more.

CHICANEAU. That's not so long.

THE COUNTESS. Alas!

CHICANEAU. And what may be your age? Your looks
  Seem young.

THE COUNTESS. Some sixty years.

CHICANEAU. Just the right age
  To plead in courts.

THE COUNTESS. Let them go on! They'll find
  They have not seen the end of me. I'll sell
  The last stitch off my back sooner than yield.

CHICANEAU. Listen! I'll tell you what you ought to do.

THE COUNTESS. I trust you, Sir, as if you were my father.

CHICANEAU. I'd have you see my judge,—

THE COUNTESS. Yes, Sir, I'll go.

CHICANEAU. Cast yourself at his feet,—

THE COUNTESS. Yes, there I'll fall,
  I'm quite resolved.

CHICANEAU. Be kind enough to hear me.

THE COUNTESS. Yes, yes, you comprehend my situation.

CHICANEAU. Have you done, Madam?

THE COUNTESS. Yes.

CHICANEAU. Then seek my judge.
  And without ceremony—

THE COUNTESS. Ah, how good
  You are!

CHICANEAU. If still you speak, I must be silent.

THE COUNTESS. You overpower me with gratitude.

CHICANEAU. Get access to my judge, and say—

THE COUNTESS. Yes.

CHICANEAU. There
  You are again! Say to him: Sir—

THE COUNTESS. Yes, Sir.

CHICANEAU. Tie me—

THE COUNTESS. I won't be tied.

CHICANEAU. What stuff and nonsense!

THE COUNTESS. I say I won't.

CHICANEAU. You have strange fancies, Madam.

THE COUNTESS. No, never.

CHICANEAU. Wait till you have heard me out.

THE COUNTESS. I'll go to law, or know the reason why.

CHICANEAU. But—

THE COUNTESS. But I'll never let them tie me, Sir—

CHICANEAU. When once a woman's head has got a craze—

THE COUNTESS. Crazy yourself!

CHICANEAU. Madam!

THE COUNTESS. Tie me, indeed!

CHICANEAU. Madam!

THE COUNTESS. The fellow grows impertinent.

CHICANEAU. But, Madam,—
THE COUNTESS. Rascal, with his dirty tricks,
    Advising me!
CHICANEAU. Madam!
THE COUNTESS. With all his talk
    About a donkey! Go, and watch your hay.
CHICANEAU. This is too much!
THE COUNTESS. Fool!
CHICANEAU. Oh, for witnesses

SCENE VIII. PETIT-JEAN, THE COUNTESS, CHICANEAU.

PETIT-JEAN. A pretty row they're making at our door!
    Go, and raise storms of this sort farther off.
CHICANEAU. Be witness, Sir—
THE COUNTESS. This gentleman's a fool.
CHICANEAU. You hear her; pray remember that expression.
PETIT-JEAN. [to THE COUNTESS.] You oughtn't to say that.
THE COUNTESS. He's a fine fellow
    To call me crazy!
PETIT-JEAN. Crazy! That was wrong.
    Why do you call her names?
CHICANEAU. 'Twas good advice.
    That I was giving her.
PETIT-JEAN. Oh, indeed!
THE COUNTESS. That I
    Should get tied up!
PETIT-JEAN. Fie, Sir!
CHICANEAU. She would not hear
    All that I had to say.
PETIT-JEAN. Fie, Ma'am!
THE COUNTESS. Am I
    To be abused by him?
CHICANEAU. A scold!
PETIT-JEAN. Peace
THE COUNTESS. Villain!
CHICANEAU. Who dares not go to law!
THE COUNTESS. What's that to you?
    Abominable swindler, meddler, thief!
PETIT-JEAN. Stop, stop!
CHICANEAU. Why that beats all! Ten thousand devils!
    Bailiffs! police!
THE COUNTESS. Oh, for a constable!
PETIT-JEAN. They must be all tied up, plaintiffs and judge.

ACT II.

SCENE I. LEANDER, L'INTIMÉ.

L'INTIMÉ. I can't do everything; there's one stroke more
    Needed; and you must play the magistrate,
    If I'm the officer. If you'll but don
    A gown and follow in my steps, you'll find
    Means to hold converse. Change that auburn wig.
    These people do not know of your existence,
    And when they come to wait upon your father,
    Day will have scarcely dawn'd. You've cause to praise
    That precious Countess whom my lucky star
    Brought just when she was wanted. Seeing me,
    She fell into the trap, and bade me serve
    A writ on Chicaneau, and summon him
    Before the Court for certain words of his,
    Whereby he wish'd to make her pass for mad,
    Too mad to be at large, with other insults
    Such as are wont to garnish writs of slander.
    But you say nothing of my fine get up.
    Don't I look like a sheriff's officer?
LEANDES. Ay, that you do!
L'INTIMÉ. I can't think how it is,
    I feel I'm twenty times the man I was.
    Well, here's the writ, and here, Sir, is your letter
    Miss Isabelle shall have it, that I promise.
    But if you'd have this marriage contract sign'd,
    You must present yourself without delay.
    Pretend to make inquiries on the matter,
    While making love under her father's nose.
LEANDER. Don't let the writ change places with the letter.
L'INTIMÉ. No. He shall have the writ, and she the "billet."
    Go in.

[L'INTIMÉ *goes and knocks at* ISABELLE's *door.*]

SCENE II. ISABELLE, L'INTIMÉ.

ISABELLE. Who knocks?
L'INTIMÉ. A friend.
    [*aside.*] The voice is hers,
    'Tis Isabelle.
ISABELLE. Who is it, Sir, you want?
L'INTIMÉ. I have a little writ here; grant me, please,
    The honour, Miss, of serving it on you.
ISABELLE. Excuse me, Sir, I cannot understand it;

My father will be here soon; speak to him.
L'INTIMÉ. Is he not then within, Miss?
ISABELLE. No, he's not.
L'INTIMÉ. The warrant, Miss, is made out in your name.
ISABELLE. You, doubtless, take me, Sir, for someone else.
    I never went to law, but know its cost;
    And if the world loved it no more than I do,
    You and your like would need some new employment.
    Farewell.
L'INTIMÉ. But, pray, allow—
ISABELLE. I'll allow nothing.
L'INTIMÉ. This is no writ.
ISABELLE. Nonsense!
L'INTIMÉ. It is a letter.
ISABELLE. That's worse.
L'INTIMÉ. But read it.
ISABELLE. No, you shall not catch me.
L'INTIMÉ. The gentleman who wrote it was—
ISABELLE. Farewell, Sir.
L'INTIMÉ. Leander.
ISABELLE. Not so loud. Who, did you say?
L'INTIMÉ. It's hard to make her listen; faith, I'm now
    Quite out of breath.
ISABELLE. Oh, pardon my surprise;
    L'Intimé, give it.
L'INTIMÉ. You'd have slamm'd the door
    Right in my face.
ISABELLE. Who would have known 'twas you
    In this disguise? Give it.
L'INTIMÉ. I like politeness.
ISABELLE. Please, give it.
L'INTIMÉ. What a plague!
    ISABELLE. Don't give it then.
    Go, take your letter with you.
L'INTIMÉ. You shall have it.
    But next time don't you be in such a hurry.

SCENE III. CHICANEAU, ISABELLE, L'INTIMÉ.

CHICANEAU. Yes, yes; she call'd me fool and thief. I've charged
    A sheriff's officer to take my thanks,
    And I'll soon serve her with a dainty dish.
    I should be vex'd were I obliged to send
    A second time, or if she sued me first.
    But who is this man talking to my daughter?
    She reads a letter: it must be a lover's.
    I will go near.
ISABELLE. Shall I believe your master?

Is he sincere?
L'INTIMÉ. He cannot sleep o' nights,
    No more than your papa; he'll—
    [*perceiving* CHICANEAU. Make you see
    How those gain nought who go to law with him.
ISABELLE. [*perceiving* CHICANEAU.] My father!
    [*to* L'INTIMÉ.] You may tell them, if they sue,
    I can defend myself.

[*Tearing the letter.*]

    Stay, look you, thus
    I treat the writ you bring me.
CHICANEAU. What is this?
        It was a writ that she was reading then.
        She'll yet do credit to her family,
        And hold her own! Come to my arms, my child!
        I'll buy you "The Complete Guide to the Law."
        But—hang it all—writs shouldn't be torn up.
ISABELLE. [*to* L'INTIMÉ.] I fear them not, and you may say as much:
    Ay, let them do their worst: it won't displease me.
CHICANEAU. Don't vex yourself, my dear.
ISABELLE. [*to* L'INTIMÉ.] Good day, Sir.

SCENE IV. CHICANEAU, L'INTIMÉ.

L'INTIMÉ. [*preparing to write.*] Now then,
    I must draw up a statement.
CHICANEAU. Sir, excuse her:
    She's ignorant; and I can piece together
    These fragments, if you'll kindly wait a moment.
L'INTIMÉ. No.
CHICANEAU. I shall soon decipher it.
L'INTIMÉ. I'll help you,
    I've got another copy.
CHICANEAU. Most obliging,
    I'm sure! Somehow, the more I look at you
    The less I'm able to recall your face,
    Tho' I know heaps of bailiffs.
L'INTIMÉ. Make inquiries.
    I'm not a bad hand at my little jobs.
CHICANEAU. May be. Who sent you?
L'INTIMÉ. A distinguish'd lady,
    Who much esteems you, and with all her heart
    Desires you to come, at my request,
    And say one word by way of reparation.
CHICANEAU. Of reparation? I have injured no one.
L'INTIMÉ. I well believe it, Sir; you are too good.

CHICANEAU. What do you want then?
L'INTIMÉ. She would have you, Sir,
    Do her the honour, before witnesses,
    Of owning her possess'd of sound good sense.
CHICANEAU. Good gracious! 'Tis my Countess!
L'INTIMÉ. At your service!
CHICANEAU. Give her my best respects.
L'INTIMÉ. I thank you, Sir.
CHICANEAU. Yes, pray assure her I have sent a bailiff
    To satisfy her claims as she deserves.
    What! Is the injured party to be punish'd?
    Let's see what song she sings. H'm—"The sixteenth
    Of January, for having falsely said,
    Prompted by evil motives, that the high
    And noble dame, the Countess of Pimbesche,
    Ought to be kept in durance as insane,
    Be't now declared th' above named Jeremy
    Shall straightway to th' aforesaid lady's house
    Betake himself, and before witnesses
    Not less than four, besides a notary,
    In a clear voice acknowledge her sound judgment."
    Sign'd, "Good." Is he your sheriff?
L'INTIMÉ. At your service.
    [*aside.*] I'll face it out in brazen impudence.
CHICANEAU. I never saw a writ sign'd "Good" before.
    Who's Mr. Good?,
L'INTIMÉ. Sir?
CHICANEAU. I say you're a rogue.
L'INTIMÉ. I beg your pardon, I'm an honest man.
CHICANEAU. The most consummate knave 'tween this and Rome.
L'INTIMÉ. 'Tis not for me to contradict you, Sir:
    But you will have to pay for defamation.
CHICANEAU. Pay? Yes, with blows.
L'INTIMÉ. You are too gentle, Sir;
    You'll pay me in good coin.
CHICANEAU. My head will burst
    If he goes on. Take that!
L'INTIMÉ. A box on th' ear!
    I'll write it down, "that the said Jeremy,
    With other outrages, struck me, a bailiff;
    And thereby knock'd my hat into the mud."
CHICANEAU. [*giving him a kick.*] Take that, too!
L'INTIMÉ. Thanks. As good as ready money!
    I want some badly. "Not content with that,
    Follow'd it up by giving me a kick."
    Bravo! "Moreover, the aforesaid Jeremy
    Tried, in a rage, to tear this present statement."
    Come, my dear Sir, this goes on splendidly.

Don't stop.

CHICANEAU. You rascal!

L'INTIMÉ. Do just what you please.

Give me the stick next, if you would oblige me.

CHICANEAU. [*holding up a stick.*] Yes, that I will, and see if you're a bailiff.

L'INTIMÉ. [*preparing to write.*] Quick, hit me then. I have four hungry children.

CHICANEAU. Forgive me! you're a bailiff, sure enough;

But the most clever man may be deceived.

I wrong'd you sadly, but will make amends:

Yes, you're a bailiff, Sir, a thorough bailiff.

Your hand: such men as you have my respect;

And my late father always brought me up

In the fear of Heav'n, and of bailiffs, Sir.

L'INTIMÉ. No, you don't beat me on such easy terms.

CHICANEAU. Don't draw up a complaint, Sir!

L'INTIMÉ. Words of insult,

A stick raised, ears box'd, and a kick!

CHICANEAU. Nay, rather

Give them me back, please.

L'INTIMÉ. They are far too precious;

I wouldn't part with them for fifty pounds.

SCENE V. LEANDER, *dressed as a magistrate,* CHICANEAU, L'INTIMÉ.

L'INTIMÉ. Here comes his Worship, in the nick of time:

Your presence, Sir, is just what we require.

This gentleman has made me a small present,

And giv'n me a tremendous box on the' ear.

LEANDER. What you, Sir?

L'INTIMÉ. Me, I say. *Item,* a kick;

Besides the names that he bestows on me.

LEANDER. And have you witnesses?

L'INTIMÉ. Put your hand here, Sir:

Feel how my ear and cheek are tingling still.

LEANDER. Ha! Taken in the act! assault and battery!

CHICANEAU. I'm in a nasty fix!

L'INTIMÉ. His daughter, too,

At least she said she was, tore up my writ,

Saying she was pleased to get it, and defied us

To do our worst.

LEANDER. [*to* L'INTIMÉ.] Then bring the daughter here.

They seem a contumacious family.

CHICANEAU. [*aside.*] These people must most surely have bewitch'd me:

May I be hang'd if I know one of them!

LEANDER. Assault a bailiff! Here's the little rebel.

SCENE VI. LEANDER, ISABELLE, CHICANEAU, L'INTIMÉ.

L'INTIMÉ.[*to* ISABELLE.] D' you recognize him?
LEANDER. Well, Miss, so it's you
    Who just now treated with supreme contempt
    Our officer, and haughtily defied us.
    Your name, please.
ISABELLE. Isabelle.
LEANDER. So. Write it down.
    Your age?
ISABELLE. Eighteen.
CHICANEAU. In fact a little more;
    But that's no matter.
LEANDER. Say, have you a husband?
ISABELLE. No, Sir.
LEANDER. You're laughing? Write down that she laugh'd.
CHICANEAU. Don't talk of husbands, Sir, to girls like her;
    You've nought to do with family affairs.
LEANDER. Write that he interrupted.
CHICANEAU. Nay, I did not
    Intend to do so. Isabelle, take care
    What you say next.
LEANDER. Pray don't alarm yourself.
    We do not wish to vex you; answer freely.
    Did not this bailiff here hand you a paper
    Just now?
ISABELLE. That's right, Sir.
CHICANEAU. Good, and so he did.
LEANDES. And did you dare to tear it up unread?
ISABELLE. I read it, Sir.
CHICANEAU. Ha! good again.
LEANDER. [*to* L'Intimé.] Write on.
    [*to* ISABELLE.] What made you tear it?
ISABELLE. Sir, I was afraid
    My father would take it to heart too much,
    And its perusal might inflame his wrath.
CHICANEAU. And you're the girl so frighten'd at the Law!
    Mere mischief.
LEANDES. So you did not tear the paper
    In scorn, or in contempt of those who sent it
    To you?
ISABELLE. I've neither anger nor contempt
    For them.
LEANDER. [*to* L'INTIMÉ.] Write that down.
CHICANEAU. She takes after me;
    She answers very well.
LEANDER. You show, however,

An evident contempt for men of law.
ISABELLE. A lawyer's gown used to offend my eyes,
But that aversion now grows somewhat less.
CHICANEAU. That's right, my child! You shall be married well,
And at no distant date—if it costs nothing.
LEANDER. You then consent to meet the claims of justice?
ISABELLE. Sir, I'll do anything to give you pleasure.
L'INTIMÉ. Sir, make her sign her name to that.
LEANDER. Will you
Confirm your promise when occasion serves?
ISABELLE. You may trust Isabelle to keep her word.
LEANDER. Sign then. That's well, justice is satisfied.
There now, will you, Sir, add your name?
CHICANEAU. With pleasure:
I sign, without a look, to all she says.
LEANDER. [aside to ISABELLE.] All has gone well. Success smiles on my wishes;
He signs a marriage contract in due form,
And his own hand will prove his condemnation.
CHICANEAU. [aside.] What is he saying to her? Charm'd no doubt
With her good sense.
LEANDER. Farewell. Be ever wise,
As you are fair. My man, escort her home.
Come, Sir.
CHICANEAU. Where now?
LEANDER. Where I shall lead you, Sir.
CHICANEAU. But where?
LEANDER. You'll soon know. In the King's name, come.
CHICANEAU. What's this?

SCENE VII. LEANDER, CHICANEAU, PETIT-JEAN.

PETIT-JEAN. I say, has anybody seen
My master? Which way went he? By the door,
Or window?
LEANDER. Don't tell me!
PETIT-JEAN. His son is vanish'd;
And for the father, deuce knows where he is.
He kept on telling me he wanted "spices;"
I, like a simpleton, ran to the pantry,
To find the pepper-box; and he, meanwhile,
Bolted.

SCENE VIII. DANDIN, *at a garret window on the roof,* LEANDER, CHICANEAU, L'INTIMÉ, PETIT-JEAN.

DANDIN. Peace! Silence in the Court, I say.
LEANDER. Good Heavens!
PETIT-JEAN. Look, he's up there on the gutter.

DANDIN. Pray, who are you? What is your business, Sirs?
Who are these gownsmen? Are you barristers?
Speak.
PETIT-JEAN. You will see, he's going to judge the cats.
DANDIN. If you have not yet seen my secretary,
Ask him if he has told me of your case.
LEANDER. I must get hold of him, and bring him down.
Keep your eyes, bailiff, on your prisoner.
PETIT-JEAN. Ho, you Sir!
LEANDER. Silence, if you love your life,
And follow me.

SCENE IX. THE COUNTESS, DANDIN, CHICANEAU, L'INTIMÉ.

DANDIN. Quick, what is your petition?
CHICANEAU. Without your order I have been arrested.
THE COUNTESS. Good gracious! Is that he among the garrets?
What is he doing there?
L'INTIMÉ. Hearing petitions.
Now is your chance.
CHICANEAU. Sir, having been assaulted,
And grievously maltreated, I come here
To make complaint to you.
THE COUNTESS. As I do also.
CHICANEAU AND THE COUNTESS. You see before you the offending party.
L'INTIMÉ. 'Faith, I will introduce my grievance too.
THE COUNTESS, CHICANEAU, AND L'INTIMÉ. Sir, I've a little writ to bring before
you.
CHICANEAU. Let us in turn prefer our several claims.
THE COUNTESS. His claim, indeed! All that he says is falsehood.
DANDIN. What wrongs have you sustain'd?
THE COUNTESS, CHICANEAU, AND L'INTIMÉ. The grossest slanders.
L'INTIMÉ. And blows, Sir; which is more than they can say.
CHICANEAU. One of your nephews is my cousin, Sir.
THE COUNTESS. My case is known to Father Cordon, Sir.
L'INTIMÉ. Sir, I'm the bastard of your surgeon-barber.
DANDIN. And what are you?
THE COUNTESS. A Countess.
L'INTIMÉ. I'm a bailiff.
CHICANEAU. And I a burgess.
DANDIN. [retiring from the garret window on the roof.] Speak, I hear you all.
CHICANEAU. Sir—
L'INTIMÉ. Look you there! He has giv'n us the slip.
THE COUNTESS. Alas!
CHICANEAU. What's this? Is the Court closed already?
I've not had time to say two words to him.

SCENE X. LEANDER, *no longer dressed as a magistrate,* CHICANEAU, THE
COUNTESS, L'INTIMÉ.

LEANDER. Be kind enough to leave us now in peace.
CHICANEAU. Mayn't I come in, Sir?
LEANDES. Not while I'm alive.
CHICANEAU. Why so? I shall not occupy an hour;
    Or two, at most.
LEANDER. There's no admittance, Sir.
THE COUNTESS. 'Tis well to shut the door upon this brawler,
    But I—
LEANDER. You cannot be admitted, Madam.
THE COUNTESS. Yes, Sir, I will.
LEANDER. Doubtful.
THE COUNTESS. I'm sure of it.
LEANDER. How? Thro' a window?
THE COUNTESS. Thro' the door.
LEANDES. We'll see.
CHICANEAU. If I must do so, I'll stay here till midnight.

SCENE XI. LEANDES, CHICANEAU, THE COUNTESS, L'INTIMÉ, PETIT-JEAN.

PETIT-JEAN. [*to* LEANDES.] No one will hear him now, do what he will.
    I've put him in a room close to the cellar.
LEANDER. One word will do as well as will a hundred,
    You cannot see my father.
CHICANEAU. Oh, indeed!
    What if I say I must? And that's the truth.

    [DANDIN *shows himself at the air-hole of the cellar.*]

    But look, Heav'n sends him to our aid once more!
LEANDES. Up from the cellar!
PETIT-JEAN. Surely he's possess'd.
CHICANEAU. Sir—
DANDIN. But for you and your impertinence
    I should not be in here.
CHICANEAU. Sir—
DANDIN. Go away,
    Don't bother.
CHICANEAU. Will you, Sir—
DANDIN. You split my head.
CHICANEAU. I've given orders—
DANDIN. Hold your tongue, I say.
CHICANEAU. That there be sent you—
DANDIN. Take him off to prison.
CHICANEAU. A cask of wine.

DANDIN. Pshaw! I'll have none of it.
CHICANEAU. Excellent muscat.
DANDIN. Please, repeat your case.
LEANDER. [to L'INTIMÉ.] We must encompass them on all sides.
THE COUNTESS. Sir,
 Nothing but lies is what you'll hear from him.
CHICANEAU. Sir, 'tis the truth, I say.
DANDIN. Zounds, let her speak.
THE COUNTESS. Pray, hear me, Sir.
DANDIN. Allow me to take breath.
THE COUNTESS. Sir—
DANDIN. I feel suffocated.
THE COUNTESS. Please, look here.
DANDIN. She'll be the death of me.
CHICANEAU. You drag me down!
 Take care, I'm falling.
PETIT-JEAN. Both, upon my word,
 Have fallen in the cellar.
LEANDER. Fly there, quick!
 Run to their help. But I intend, at least,
 Now Chicaneau's inside, to keep him there
 Till morning. L'Intimé, take care of him.
L'INTIMÉ. The air-hole must be watch'd.
LEANDER. Go, I'll do that.

SCENE XII. THE COUNTESS, LEANDES.

THE COUNTESS. The wretch will prepossess him in his favour.

[*She speaks through the cellar air-hole.*]

 Pray, believe nothing that he tells you, Sir;
 He is a liar, and has no witnesses.
LEANDER. What's that you say to them? They may be dying
 For aught we know.
THE COUNTESS. He'll make him swallow all
 He chooses. Let me enter.
LEANDER. No, you shan't.
THE COUNTESS. I see the muscat wine works upon you,
 As much as on your father's inclination.
 Patience, I will protest in legal form
 Against the judge, also against the cask.
LEANDER. Go then, and let us have a little peace.
 What fools! I never met such company.

SCENE XIII. DANDIN, LEANDER, L'INTIMÉ.

L'INTIMÉ. Where are you running, Sir? You'll hurt yourself,
    Limping along like that
DANDIN. I want to judge.
LEANDER. No, father; you must let your wounds be dress'd.
    Quick, fetch a surgeon.
DANDIN. Bring him into Court.
LEANDER. Stop, father, stop!
DANDIN. Oh! I can see what's up;
    You mean to make of me just what you please,
    Casting off filial reverence and regard;
    You will not let me judge a single case.
    Have done, and take this bag; be quick.
LEANDER. There, gently,
    My father. We must find some compromise.
    If judging is your only joy in life,
    And you feel bound to sit upon the Bench,
    There is no need to leave your house for that;
    Fulfil your favorite office here with us.
DANDIN. Don't ridicule a judge's dignity:
    I do not wish to be a dummy, Sir.
LEANDER. Nay, you shall judge, and that without appeal,
    In civil causes as in criminal.
    You can hold sittings twice a day, and all
    That passes in our midst be brought before you.
    A servant brings a dirty glass,—you fine him;
    Or if he breaks one, you award a whipping.
DANDIN. That's something. It deserves consideration.
    But who's to pay me for my services?
LEANDER. Their wages will be your security.
DANDIN. That's to the point. Your scheme seems feasible.
LEANDER. And as regards a neighbour—

SCENE XIV. DANDIN, LEANDER, L'INTIMÉ, PETIT-JEAN.

PETIT-JEAN. Stop, there! Catch him!
LEANDER. [to L'INTIMÉ.] Ah! Have you let my prisoner escape?
L'INTIMÉ. No fear of that.
PETIT-JEAN. I am undone—your dog—
    Ginger—has just run off with a fat capon,
    And eaten it. One can keep nothing from him.
LEANDER. Good, here's a case for him to try. Help! Run!
    All join in the pursuit, and catch the thief.
DANDIN. No noise. Arrest th' offender quietly.
LEANDER. This household robber must be judged severely,
    And made a notable example, father.

DANDIN. With due formalities I wish th' affair
　To be conducted, with opposing counsel;
　And there are none.
LEANDER. Well, we must make some then.
　There are your porter and your secretary;
　They will prove first-rate advocates, I fancy;
　They're very ignorant.
L'INTIMÉ. Oh, not at all, Sir;
　I'll send him fast asleep as well as any.
PETIT-JEAN. Don't expect much from me, for I know nothing.
LEANDER. This is your first case. We'll prepare it for you.
PETIT-JEAN. But I can't read.
LEANDER. Then you shall have a prompter.
DANDIN. Let's go, and make us ready. We must close
　Our eyes to bribes, our ears to all corruption.
　You, Master Petit-Jean, are for the plaintiff;
　And Master L'Intimé for the defendant.

ACT III.

SCENE I. LEANDER, CHICANEAU, THE PROMPTER.

CHICANEAU. Yes, Sir, 'twas thus, I say, they treated me.
　I knew not either magistrate or tipstaff.
　'Tis true, each word I speak.
LEANDER. Yes, I believe you;
　But were I you, I'd let the matter drop;
　You should not drive them to extremities,
　Or you will do yourself more harm than them.
　You've spent three quarters of your whole estate
　Already, Sir, in stuffing lawyers' bags;
　And in a vain pursuit that only harms you—
CHICANEAU. Indeed, you give me excellent advice,
　And I intend, ere long, to profit by it.
　But, first, I crave your kindly offices.
　Since your good father will give audience soon
　To suitors, I will fetch my daughter hither;
　Let her be question'd, she will speak the truth,
　And answer better than myself can do.
LEANDER. Go then; when you come back, you shall have justice.
THE PROMPTER. Queer fellow, this!

SCENE II. LEANDER, THE PROMPTER.

LEANDER. My scheme's perhaps a strange one;
　But my poor father's craze is desperate,
　And we must get up something to deceive him.
　I have another purpose, too, and wish

This madman, so outrageously litigious,
To lose his suit. But here come all our people.

SCENE III. DANDIN, LEANDER, L'INTIMÉ AND PETIT-JEAN, *dressed as advocates,* THE PROMPTER.

DANDIN. Pray, who are you?
LEANDER. These are the advocates.
DANDIN. [*to the Prompter.*] And you?
THE PROMPTER. I come t' assist their memories.
DANDIN. I see. And you?
LEANDER. I represent the public.
DANDIN. Begin then.
THE PROMPTER. Gentlemen—
PETIT-JEAN. Don't speak so loud;
    For, if you prompt like that, they can't hear me.
    Gentlemen—
DANDIN. Put your cap on.
PETIT-JEAN. Oh, my lord—
DANDIN. Put on your cap, I say.
PETIT-JEAN. I know my place.
DANDIN. Don't put it on, then.
PETIT-JEAN. [*putting on his cap.*] Gentlemen—
    [*to the Prompter.*] Be quiet;
    I know the first part of my speech all right.
    Gentlemen, when I carefully observe
    The mutability of mundane matters.
    And see amidst the various tribes of men
    Not one fix'd star, but many wandering orbs;
    When I behold the Cæsars and their greatness;
    When I behold the sun, and view the moon;
    When I behold the rule of Babybonia[1]
    Pass from the Serpians[2] to the Nacedonians;[3]
    When I see Lome[4] change from prespotic[5] pow'r
    To memocratic,[6] thence to monarchy;
    When I survey Japan—
L'INTIMÉ. When will the fellow
    Have done surveying?
PETIT-JEAN. Why this interruption?
    I'll say no more.
DANDIN. You meddling advocate,
    Why can't you let him finish his exordium?

---

[1] Babylonia.
[2] Persians.
[3] Macedonians.
[4] Rome.
[5] Despotic.
[6] Democratic.

I was quite feverish with desire to hear
How from Japan he'd come back to his capon,
When you thrust in your frivolous remark.
Counsel, proceed.
PETIT-JEAN. Ah, now I've lost the thread.
LEANDER. Courage! Go on, you've made a fine beginning;
But why d' you let your arms hang at your side
Like that, and stand stock still like any statue?
Come, rouse yourself, and show a little life.
PETIT-JEAN. [*moving his arms up and down.*] When—when I see—I see—
LEANDER. Say what you see.
PETIT-JEAN. Zounds, I can't hunt two hares at once, you know
THE PROMPTER. We read—
PETIT-JEAN. We read—
THE PROMPTER. In th' Metamorphoses—
PETIT-JEAN. Eh?
THE PROMPTER. That the Metempsy—
PETIT-JEAN. The Metempsy—
THE PROMPTER.—chosis—
PETIT-JEAN. The chosis—
THE PROMPTER. Donkey!
PETIT-JEAN. Donkey.
THE PROMPTER. Stop!
PETIT-JEAN. Stop.
THE PROMPTER. Silly idiot!
PETIT-JEAN. Silly idiot.
THE PROMPTER. Dolt!
PETIT-JEAN. Dolt.
THE PROMPTER. Plague upon you!
PETIT-JEAN. Plague upon yourself!
Look at that fellow with his lantern jaws!
Go to the deuce!
DANDIN. And you, come to the point;
Tell me the facts.
PETIT-JEAN. Why beat about the bush?
They make me talk in words a fathom long,
In words that reach from here to Jericho.
For my part I've no need of such ado
In saying that a mastiff stole a capon,
(Indeed there's nothing that he won't run off with,)
And ate it up,—the finest in the yard.
The first time that I find him there again,
His trial shall be short, I'll crack his skull.
LEANDER. A fine conclusion,—worthy of the prologue!
PETIT-JEAN. It's plain enough, find fault with it who may.
DANDIN. Call witnesses.
LEANDER. That's easier said than done,
For witnesses cost dear, or won't come forward.

PETIT-JEAN. We've got some, all the same,—beyond reproach.

DANDIN. Produce them, then.

PETIT-JEAN. I have them in my pocket:
    Look here, I've got the capon's head and legs,
    See then, and judge.

L'INTIMÉ. Nay, I object.

DANDIN. All right,
    What's your objection?

L'INTIMÉ. They're from Maine, my lord.

DANDIN. Ah, true; they hatch them by the dozen there.

L'INTIMÉ. My lord—

DANDIN. Will you be long, Sir? Tell me that.

L'INTIMÉ. I really cannot say.

DANDIN. At least, he's honest.

L'INTIMÉ. [*rising to a scream.*] Whate'er can daunt a prisoner at the bar,
    All that to mortals shows most terrible,
    Fortune appears to have array'd against us,
    In eloquence and partisanship. For
    While on the one hand the deceased's renown
    Alarms me, on the other my opponent
    With practised tongue confounds.

DANDIN. Pray, Sir, subdue
    Your own o'erpowering accents, if you please.

L'INTIMÉ. [*in an ordinary tone.*] I will: I've many others.
    [*in a soft tone of voice.*] But howe'er
    His sounding periods fill me with mistrust,
    And the deceased one's fame; yet still, my lord,
    I rest my hopes on your impartial mind.
    Before great Dandin innocence is bold,
    Before this Cato of our Norman soil;
    This Sun of Justice that is never dim;
    Victrix causa diis placuit, sed victa Catoni.

DANDIN. Truly, he argues well.

L'INTIMÉ. So without fear
    I speak, and advocate my righteous cause.
    In Aristotle's work on "Politics "
    It has been said full well—

DANDIN. The question, Sir,
    Concerns a capon, and not politics.

L'INTIMÉ. Yes, but the Stagirite's authority
    Would prove that good and evil—

DANDIN. I maintain
    That Aristotle has no *locus standi* here.
    Come to the facts.

L'INTIMÉ. Pausanias in his book—

DANDIN. Discuss the facts.

L'INTIMÉ. Rebuffi—

DANDIN. Facts, I say,

L'INTIMÉ. The great James—
DANDIN. Facts, facts, facts!
L'INTIMÉ. Harmenopul—
DANDIN. I will sum up.
L'INTIMÉ. You are so quick, my lord.
> [*speaking rapidly.*] The facts are these. A dog invades a kitchen,
> And finds a capon there of good proportions.
> Now, he for whom I speak is very hungry,
> He against whom I speak lies ready pluck'd,
> Then he whose cause I plead, with stealthy step
> Draws near, and grabs him against whom I've spoken.
> A warrant's issued, he's arrested, counsel
> Are call'd, a day is fix'd, I am to speak,
> I speak, and I have spoken, There,—I've done!
DANDIN. Tut, tut! A pretty way to state a case!
> His pace is slow and stately while he utters
> Irrelevant remarks; but, when he comes
> To facts, he gallops.
L'INTIMÉ. The best part came first.
DANDIN. Nay, worst. That's not the proper way to plead.
> What say the public?
LEANDER. Quite in th' latest fashion.
L'INTIMÉ. [*in an impassioned tone.*]
> What happens next? They come,—how do they come?
> They chase my client, break into a house,—
> Whose house? Your house, my lord,—our judge's house;
> The cellar is invaded, where we fled;
> We are accused of theft and brigandage,
> Dragg'd out, and given over to our foes,
> To Master Petit-Jean. You'll bear me out,
> My lord, that in the Digest *Si quis canis,*—
> De *vi*—and paragraph *caponibus,*
> The law condemns an outrage of this kind;
> And even were it true my client Ginger
> Had eaten all or part of the said capon,
> All he had done before should be consider'd
> In mitigation of his punishment.
> When has my client merited rebuke?
> Has not your house by him been safely guarded?
> When has he fail'd to bark at robbers' footsteps?
> Witness three proctors, who by Ginger here
> Had their gowns torn. See, I produce the pieces.
> Will you have other proofs of his good conduct?
PETIT-JEAN. Ah, Master Adam—
L'INTIMÉ. Peace!
PETIT-JEAN. But, L'Intimé—
L'INTIMÉ. Peace!
PETIT-JEAN. You are growing hoarse.

L'INTIMÉ. Leave me alone.
DANDIN. Compose yourself, and finish.
L'INTIMÉ. [*in a drawling tone.*] Since I may,—
    Take breath,—and am forbidden,—to prolong,—
    My speech,—I will without prevarication
    Compendiously express, explain, unfold
    Before your eyes the transcendental truth
    Of this my cause, and of the facts involved.
DANDIN. Let him say all, and say it twenty times,
    Rather than such abridgment. Be you human,
    Or fiend incarnate, end—or Heav'n confound you!
L'INTIMÉ. I've nearly done.
DANDIN. Ah!
L'INTIMÉ. Ere the world was made—
DANDIN. Let us get on, Sir, to the deluge.
L'INTIMÉ. Ere
    The world was made, before it was created,
    The world and all the universe lay buried
    In the abyss of matter, Earth and Air,
    Water and Fire,—all the elements,
    Heap'd in confusion, swallow'd up in space;
    A shapeless, indistinguishable mass
    Form'd one vast chaos, where no order reign'd;
    Unus erat toto Naturæ vultus in orbe,
    Quem Græci dixere Chaos, rudis indigestaque moles.

[DANDIN *goes to sleep, and tumbles off his chair.*]

LEANDER. Oh, father! What a fall!
PETIT-JEAN. He's fast asleep!
LEANDER. Father, wake up.
PETIT-JEAN. Sir, are you dead?
LEANDER. My father!
DANDIN. Well, well, what is it? What a man he is!
    I've never had so sound a nap before.
LEANDER. Give sentence, father.
DANDIN. To the galleys with him!
LEANDER. A dog sent to the galleys!
DANDIN. Faith, I know
    Nothing about the matter. My head's full
    Of chaos and confusion.
L'INTIMÉ. [*exhibiting some puppies.*] Come, poor children,
    Come, cruel hearts would leave you fatherless;
    Come, let your innocence for mercy plead.
    Yes, here you may behold our misery;
    Make us not orphans, give us back our father,
    Our father, he to whom we owe our life,
    Our father, who—

DANDIN. Quick, quick, take them away.

L'INTIMÉ. Our father—

DANDIN. What a hubbub! Take them off;
    They're messing all the place.

L'INTIMÉ. See, we are weeping.

DANDIN. My heart already melts with sympathy;
    Oh! 'tis a sight to touch a father's heart!
    I'm terribly perplex'd. The truth is clear;
    Th' offence is proved; he has himself confess'd it.
    But, if he be condemn'd, how hard the fate
    Of these poor children, left to charity!
    I've an engagement,—no one must disturb me.

SCENE IV. DANDIN, LEANDER, CHICANEAU, ISABELLE, PETIT-JEAN,
L'INTIMÉ.

CHICANEAU. My lord—

DANDIN. [*to* PETIT-JEAN *and* L'INTIMÉ.] Yes, I will hear you, and you only.
    [*to* CHICANEAU.] Good day. But tell me, please, who is that child?

CHICANEAU. That is my daughter.

DANDIN. Quick, then, call her back.

ISABELLE. You are engaged.

DANDIN. No matter, I assure you,
    [*to* CHICANEAU.] You might have told me that you were her father.

CHICANEAU. Sir—

DANDIN. Let her speak, she knows your business best.
    [*to* ISABELLE.] Speak, dear—How pretty, and what charming eyes!
    But that's not all. You must be wise as well.
    It does me good to see such youth and beauty.
    I've been a gay young fellow in my day,
    And been much talk'd about.

ISABELLE. I well believe it.

DANDIN. Tell me, now, who you wish should lose his cause.

ISABELLE. No one.

DANDIN. For you I will do anything.
    Speak.

ISABELLE. I am sure I'm much obliged to you.

DANDIN. Hast ever witness'd anybody tortured?

ISABELLE. No, and I trust I never shall, my lord.

DANDIN. If you would like it, you shall see it done.

ISABELLE. Ah! could one ever see poor wretches suffer?

DANDIN. It serves to pass away an hour or two.

CHICANEAU. My lord, I come to tell you—

LEANDER. I can state
    The whole affair, my father, in two words;
    It is about a marriage. You must know
    That all is settled, and your sanction only
    Is wanting. Both the lovers long to wed,

The father to his daughter's wish consents.
Will you confirm the contract?
DANDIN. [*resuming his seat.*] Let them marry
Without delay, to-morrow if they please,
To-day if need be.
LEANDER. See, my father's yours,
Greet him, my love.
CHICANEAU. How's this?
DANDIN. What myst'ry's here?
LEANDER. Your judgment is precisely carried out.
DANDIN. I can't revoke the sentence I've pronounced.
CHICANEAU. But surely you'll consult my daughter's wishes.
LEANDER. By all means. Let fair Isabelle decide.
CHICANEAU. Well, are you dumb? It is your turn to speak.
ISABELLE. I do not dare to appeal against the judgment.
CHICANEAU. I'll do it, then.
LEANDER. [*showing him a paper.*]
Look at this writing, Sir.
You will not challenge your own signature?
CHICANEAU. What is it, pray?
LEANDER. A marriage contract, Sir,
All duly sign'd and seal'd.
CHICANEAU. I have been trick'd,
But I'll have satisfaction. This shall lead
To twenty lawsuits. If you get my daughter,
You shall not get my money.
LEANDER. Have I ask'd it?
Give me your daughter, I want nothing else.
CHICANEAU. Ah!
LEANDER. Father, are you pleased with your day's work?
DANDIN. Right well. Let suits flow in abundantly,
And I will pass my life with you, content.
The advocates, however, must not be
So lengthy. What about the culprit?
LEANDER. Father,
Pardon him. Let us all rejoice to-day.
DANDIN. Well, let him go.
[*to* ISABELLE.] For your sake, dear, he's free.
I'll take a holiday, then try new cases.

CPSIA information can be obtained at www.ICGtesting.com
Printed in the USA
LVOW11s2057031114

411809LV00001B/242/P